Copyright © 202_

All Rights Reserved.

No part of this publication may be reproduced, distributed, or transmitted in any form or by any means. Including photocopying, recording, or other electronic ormechanical methods, without the prior written permission of the publisher, expect in the case of the brief quotations embodied in critical reviews and certain other non-commercial uses permitted by copyright law.

I Spy with my little eye Something beginning with ...

Accordion

I Spy with my little eye Something beginning with ...

I Spy with my little eye Something beginning with ...

Dye eggs

I Spy with my little eye Something beginning with ...

I Spy with my little eye Something beginning with ...

Flower

I Spy with my little eye Something beginning with ...

Gifts

I Spy with my little eye Something beginning with ...

Hatch

I Spy with my little eye Something beginning with ...

Ice cream

I Spy with my little eye Something beginning with ...

J

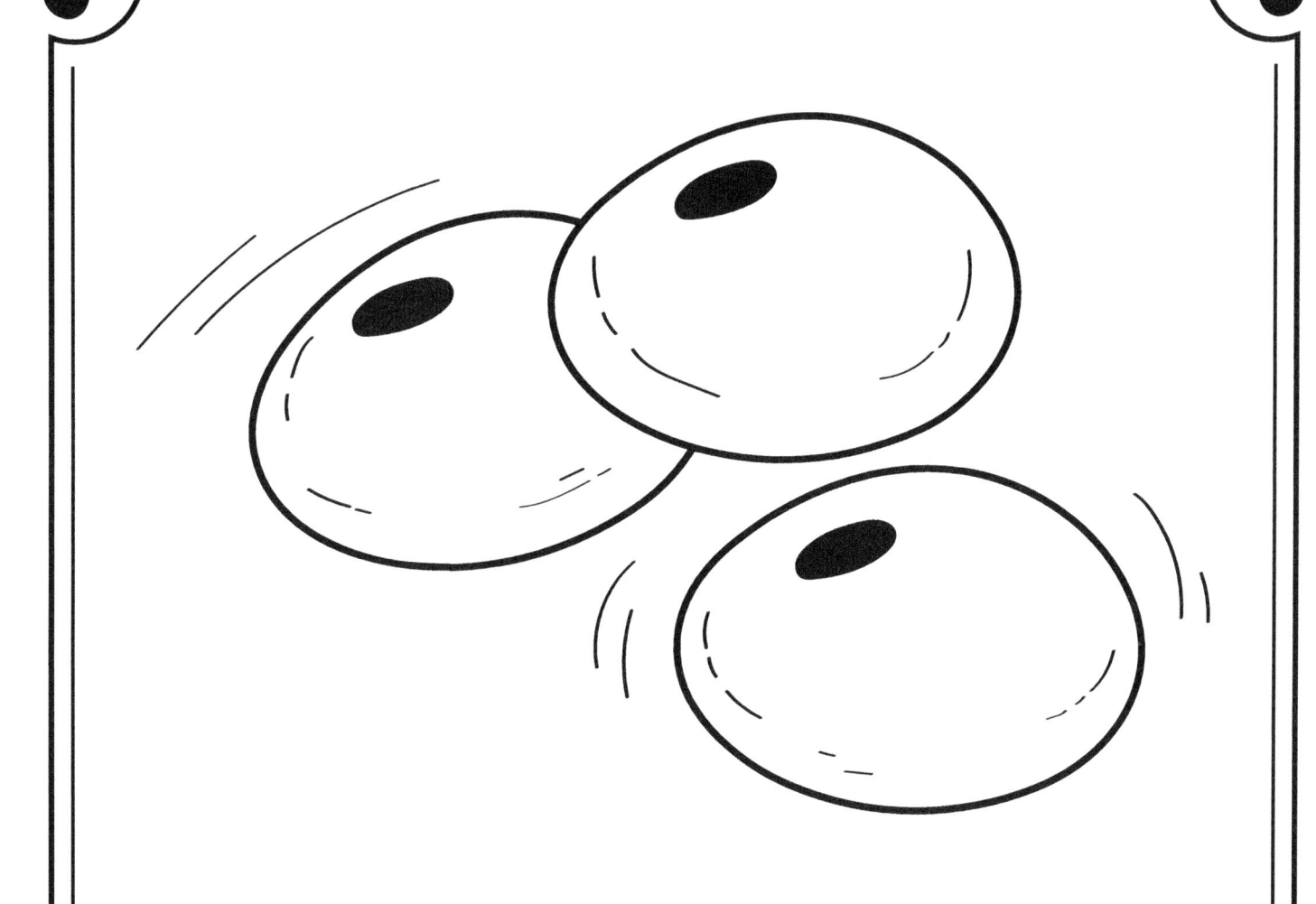

Jelly beans

I Spy with my little eye Something beginning with ...

K

Kite

I Spy with my little eye
Something beginning with ...

L

Lamb

I Spy with my little eye Something beginning with ...

M

Magic

I Spy with my little eye Something beginning with ...

N

Nest

I Spy with my little eye Something beginning with ...

O

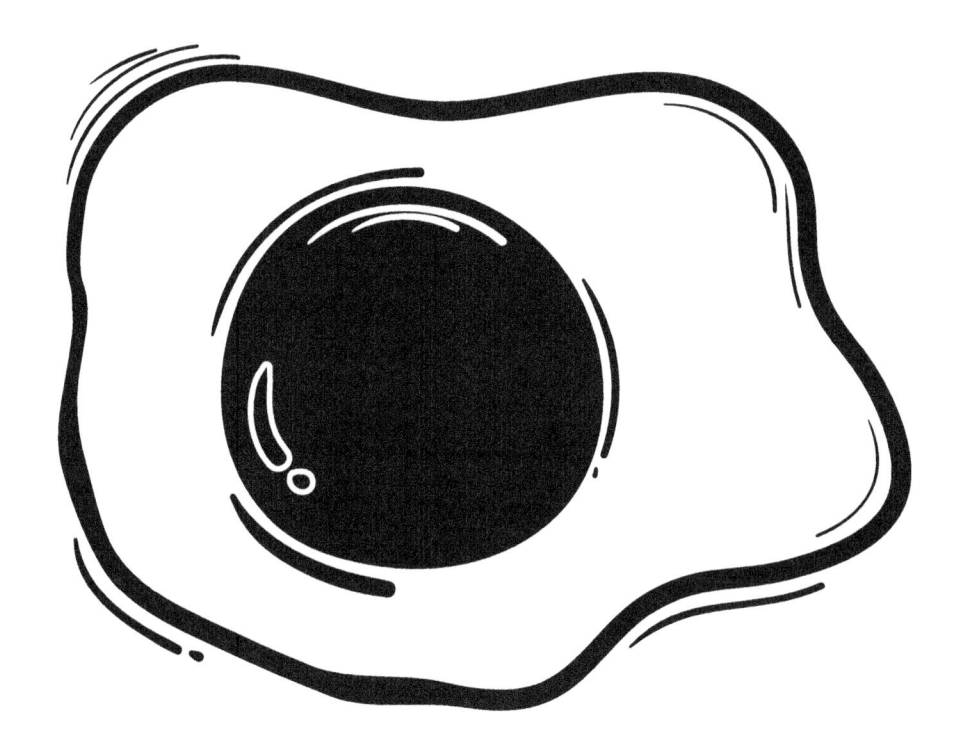

Omelette

I Spy with my little eye Something beginning with ...

P

Paint

I Spy with my little eye Something beginning with ...

Q

Quill

I Spy with my little eye Something beginning with ...

R

Rabbit

I Spy with my little eye Something beginning with ...

S

Sweet candy

I Spy with my little eye Something beginning with ...

T

Treasure

I Spy with my little eye Something beginning with ...

U

Unicorn

I Spy with my little eye Something beginning with ...

V

Violin

I Spy with my little eye Something beginning with ...

w

Wreath
with eggs

I Spy with my little eye Something beginning with ...

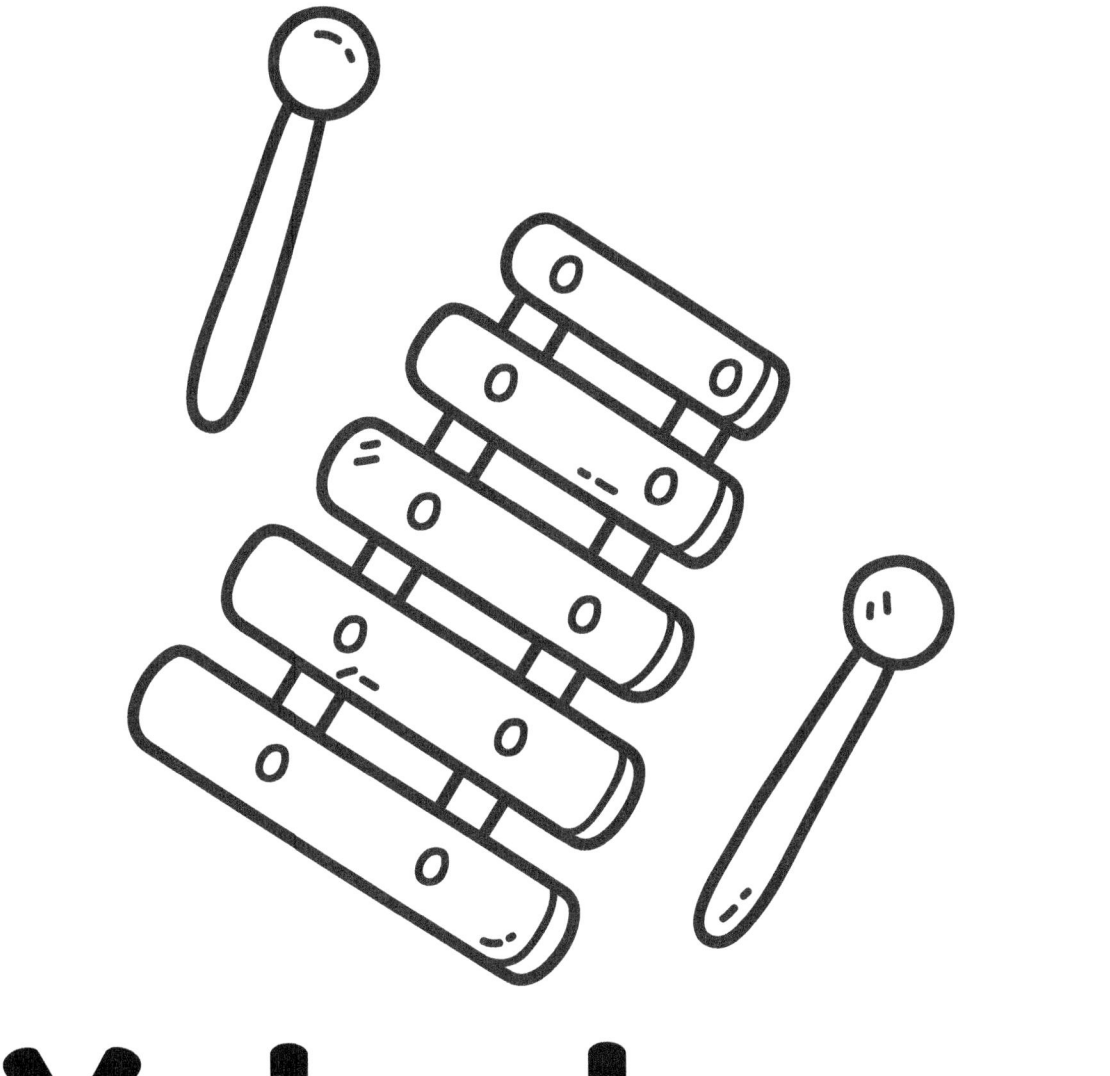

Xylophone

I Spy with my little eye Something beginning with ...

Y

Yarn

I Spy with my little eye
Something beginning with ...

z

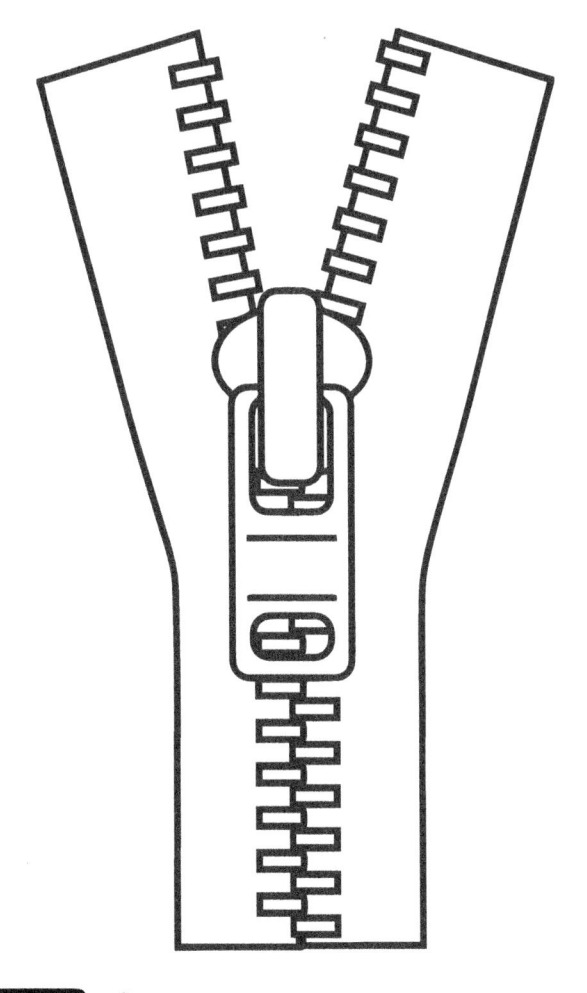

Zipper

HAPPY EASTER

I hope you enjoyed
Support our work by leaving us
Good Feedback!
Discover more fun books in
Our store "Flora Wenna"

Printed in Great Britain
by Amazon